CHARLES LINDBERGH

Crete-Monee High School
Information Resource Center
Crete, Illinois

BY ANNE SCHRAFF

Development: Kent Publishing Services, Inc.

Design and Production: Signature Design Group

SADDLEBACK EDUCATIONAL PUBLISHING

Three Watson

Irvine, CA 92618-2767

Web site: www.sdlback.com

Photo Credits: pages 32, 52, 61, Library of Congress

ISBN-13: 978-1-59905-250-2

ISBN-10: 1-59905-250-4

eBook: 978-1-60291-611-1

Printed in China

1 2 3 4 5 6 10 09 08 07

TABLE OF CONTENTS

CHAPTER 1

Twenty-five-year-old Charles Lindbergh flew a plane alone non-stop across the Atlantic Ocean. This adventure took place on May 21, 1927. His daring journey from New York to Paris was the first flight of this kind in history. The flight brought the world of **aviation** dramatically into the public eye. Air travel was rare and unusual before this. Lindbergh launched the age of commercial aviation.

Charles Augustus Lindbergh was born on February 4, 1902, in Detroit, because he loved being with his mother. She made the lessons exciting. But then he was sent to public school, and he hated it. He disliked the other children. He found the lessons boring. Although he was bright, he did poorly.

In 1913 when Charles was eleven, he was enrolled in a private school—Sidwell Friends School. It was better than public school, but still Charles did not like it. The other children made fun of his name. They called him "limburger cheese," or just "cheese." Charles avoided his classmates and did not join in any games.

Sometimes Charles's father took him to Washington to sit in on the sessions in Congress. Charles saw the president. He was proud that his father was such an important man, making speeches and passing laws.

One day, Charles heard the roar of an engine that was different than anything he had heard before. He ran to his bedroom window to see an airplane with two sets of wings flying over the treetops. It was the first plane the five-year-old had ever seen. He was thrilled. The image of that little plane stayed in his mind.

At age seven, Charles got a Savage .22 caliber repeating rifle. He shot a duck fifty feet away. He was an excellent **marksman**. He swam and fished, and grew into a rugged, self-reliant boy.

Charles's parents were not happy together. But, they did not want to get a divorce for fear of hurting their son. Still, Charles noticed their unhappiness, and it made him sad.

Until he was eight, Charles was home-schooled by his mother. He enjoyed this

States Congress as a **Republican**. He was now away from the family for long periods because he worked in Washington, D.C.

Young Charles was very shy. He had no friends, except for his dogs. He loved to collect things. He had collections of stones, arrowheads, cigar bands, coins, and stamps. He was happiest when he was alone with his dog, roaming through the woods or having adventures.

He built a raft and **poled** himself down the Mississippi in it. He also built stilts and a garden hut behind the house. He was a clever boy. He noticed his mother had a hard time getting ice from the river for her icebox. So, Charles built a series of planks and **pulleys** to bring chunks of ice from the river right into the family kitchen. Charles loved animals, and he trained a wild chipmunk to be a pet.

Michigan. His family was Swedish, English, Irish, and Scottish. His mother, Evangeline, was a schoolteacher. His father, Charles, was a lawyer, realtor, and also, a member of the **United States House of Representatives**. Evangeline was seventeen years younger than her husband.

Charles was raised in Little Falls, Minnesota along the Mississippi River. The family was wealthy with a cook, a maid, and a **coachman**. As a baby and small child, Charles spent most of his time outside in the **brisk** Minnesota weather. His father wanted to toughen him up. He wanted Charles to be a rugged boy.

The Lindberghs raised cattle, hogs, sheep, chickens, horses, and pigeons. Charles always had a dog. He loved dogs all his life. In 1906 when Charles was four, his father was elected to the United

CHAPTER 2

When Charles was twelve, his father took him to the **Aeronautical** Trials at Ft. Myers, Virginia. Six airplanes took off and landed. Charles watched with great excitement. He made up his mind that day that he would fly a plane someday.

Charles also traveled to the Panama Canal. He saw alligators, monkeys, lizards, tarantulas, coral snakes, and sharks. He was delighted to see all the exotic creatures. It was the beginning of his deep love for nature.

In 1913 the Lindberghs got a Model T Ford. Charles then learned to drive it. He did exercises to lengthen his legs so he could reach the controls. Soon he was driving all over in the Model T as well as on a motorcycle.

Charles entered Little Falls High School for a while. Then, his mother had to go to California. Although Charles had no driver's license, he drove his mother and himself from Minnesota to California.

They stayed in California, and Charles entered 11th grade at Redondo Union High School in Redondo Beach, California. Mother and son took motor trips all over southern California. Charles loved the ocean beaches.

In 1917 Charles and his mother returned to Little Falls. Fifteen-year-old Charles played a major role in running the farm, bookkeeping, and tending the **livestock**. Most of the time, his father was in Washington.

At this time, the United States was getting involved in World War I. The war was being fought between England, France, and Russia against Germany and its allies.

Charles's father made speeches against American involvement in the war. He believed all wars were stupid and evil. He thought that a country should avoid them at all cost. Charles heard many of his father's bitter speeches against the war. Therefore, these ideas were planted firmly in the boy's mind. As Charles grew older, these attitudes would shape his life.

In his last year of high school, Charles did well in physics and mechanical drawing. But he failed everything else. It looked like he would not be getting his high school diploma.

Then, the school district announced that because World War I was raging, food products were in desperate need. They said that any boy who went to work on a farm producing food would automatically get his high school diploma.

So in June 1918, Charles's work on the farm gained him his high school diploma. At the time, he was raising chickens and lambs. He was also mending fences, cutting trees, and clearing the land. All the time, he was dreaming of becoming a pilot as soon as he could.

The Lindbergh farm was sold then. Charles Lindbergh enrolled at the University of Wisconsin in Madison,

Wisconsin. Charles's parents were no longer living together. So, his mother moved to Madison, too, while he attended college there.

Once again, Charles Lindbergh disliked his classes and made no friends. The only activity he liked was the Reserve Officers Training Corps. He became a **cadet**. He was very good with pistols and rifles. He wrote letters to many flying schools. He hoped to quit college and learn to fly.

In February 1922 he quit college and joined the Nebraska Aircraft Corporation. He worked on planes. Finally, he went on his first flight in a Lincoln Standard Tourabout. He was thrilled to be riding in the cockpit, and soon he was a pilot. He found the actual flying and the take off easy. But he had a hard time learning to land smoothly.

Lindbergh began doing stunts on the wings of planes. Sometimes he would stand on the wing. His feet would be strapped down, and the pilot would fly loops. Lindbergh earned the name "Daredevil Lindbergh." By mid-May 1922, Lindbergh had eight hours of flying experience in a Fokker **biplane**. The other pilots nicknamed him "Slim" because he was tall and **lanky**.

Lindbergh wanted to experience jumping from a plane with a parachute. So, in 1922 he got out of the plane at an altitude of about 2,000 feet. He crawled from the cockpit and crept along the wing until he jumped. The parachute blossomed overhead as he sailed down.

Now, Lindbergh wanted his own plane. He set about getting it.

CHAPTER 3

Charles Lindbergh saved enough money to buy a 90 horsepower Curtiss Jenny. This plane was capable of going seventy mph (miles per hour). The plane cost five hundred dollars. Lindbergh flew solo in the plane. He almost crash landed! But by the end of the day, he mastered the technique of landing.

In the summer of 1922, Lindbergh flew all over the United States. He took passengers for rides to earn money. In 1926 he became an airmail pilot on the St. Louis to Chicago mail route. He often flew through thick fog and **treacherous** weather conditions.

Now twenty-five, Lindbergh heard of the Orteig Prize. Raymond Orteig was a French businessman. He was offering $25,000 to any flier or group of fliers who could cross the Atlantic Ocean from New York to Paris, or Paris to New York non-stop. Lindbergh was excited about the offer. He believed he could do it.

Charles Lindbergh did not have enough money to **accomplish** this goal. He did not have a plane that could make the journey. So, he looked for financial **backers**. He spoke to a group of interested men in St. Louis, Missouri. They provided the money.

Ryan Aircraft Company, a small company in San Diego, California, was chosen to build the plane. The plane would be called the *Spirit of St. Louis* in honor of the backers.

By mid-April 1927, a single engine Ryan monoplane was wheeled out of the Ryan factory. On April 28 at Dutch flats, south of San Diego, Lindbergh took the plane up. For the next two weeks he tested the plane. He cruised at 130 mph On May 10, Lindbergh piloted the *Spirit of St. Louis* to New York to make the historical flight.

On the morning of the flight, Lindbergh arrived at the **hangar** at 3 a.m. The *Spirit of St. Louis* weighed 5,250 pounds. It had a top speed of 130 mph and a capacity of 400 gallons of fuel. It had a range of 4,000 miles. It was 3,500 miles from New York to Paris.

It was raining when Lindbergh got into the cockpit, buckled his seat belt, and adjusted his goggles. Men pushed on the wing **struts** to get the plane moving. The wheels were up briefly. Then, the *Spirit* splashed in a mud puddle. Then, the plane was up for good, and Lindbergh pulled back on the **throttle**. He was on his way. It was 7:54 Eastern Daylight Time, May 20, 1927.

At 9:30 a.m., the small silver plane cleared Rhode Island. The Atlantic Ocean lay ahead. Lindbergh was used to flying over land, guiding himself by landmarks. Now, there would be miles of ocean waves below him.

To save weight, Lindbergh rejected a radio. All he had was a compass, a **sextant**, and a chart. He relied on the stars overhead to guide him.

After passing over Newfoundland, Lindbergh leveled off at 10,500 feet. He grew very cold. Sleet was **pelting** the plane. He could see that the wings were icing over. Lindbergh dropped altitude slowly to melt the ice. Thunderheads, like huge white mountains, lay before him.

He wove his little plane carefully through the clouds. Lindbergh was **assailed** by strange feelings. He was not sure if he was asleep or awake. He had to fight to stay awake.

At the 18th hour of the flight, Lindbergh passed the point of no return. It would now have taken longer to go back to New York than to fly on to Paris. Lindbergh had brought along five sandwiches for the journey: two with ham, two with beef, and one with egg. They were all wrapped in grease-proof paper. But, he had no appetite. He did not even feel thirsty.

Lindbergh stared at his instrument panel and was struck with confusion. He flexed his muscles, stamped his feet, and bounced in the cockpit to revive himself. He leaned from the cockpit and let the cold air whip him. Whenever Lindbergh started to fall asleep, the plane rattled. This **startled** him awake.

In the 27th hour, Lindbergh saw something below; perhaps it was land or a boat. He dropped altitude until he was only fifty feet above some fishing **trawlers**. He was excited to see people after so many hours alone. Lindbergh shouted to them and waved, but they made no sign in return.

An hour later, Lindbergh saw many people below. At first he did not trust his own eyesight. Then, he realized he was going across the southwest coast of Ireland. People from the village below looked up and waved.

In the 31st hour, he flew over Cornwall, England. Then, he flew across the French coast. He passed over Cherbourg Harbor at 9:52 p.m. Charles Lindbergh saw the famous Eiffel Tower and the lights of Paris. He had made it.

The *Spirit of St. Louis* set down at LeBourget Airfield in Paris in the darkness of Saturday, May 21, 1927. Charles Lindbergh had flown from New York to Paris in 33 and 1/2 hours. It was 10:24 p.m. European time.

From out of the darkness, Lindbergh heard his name being chanted. What the young American pilot did not yet realize was that his life would never be normal again. He had no idea of the price he would have to pay for his courageous deed. His personal privacy was gone. He had opened the world of aviation to the world by crossing the Atlantic. Now, the world wanted to own him.

The wildly enthusiastic crowds caught sight of the handsome, young American with the shy, endearing grin. Their reaction was near **hysterical**. He was celebrated in the capitals of Europe and surrounded by adoring fans.

Charles Lindbergh, now called "The Lone Eagle," finally returned to the United States. When he arrived, there was one of the largest parades New York had ever seen.

CHAPTER 4

Charles Lindbergh received two million pieces of fan mail. Five thousand of the letters contained poetry written about his flight. He also received gifts. Streets, towns, mountains, and newborn babies were named after him. He had become the most famous young man on earth.

Congress voted to give him the Medal of Honor. In the summer of 1927, he made an air tour of the United States in the *Spirit of St. Louis*. Everywhere he went, cheering crowds followed him.

Lindbergh already had contracts with oil and sparkplug companies and Wright Aeronautical Corporation. He was offered thousands to **endorse** other products. Young ladies flocked to the handsome, unmarried Lindbergh.

Up until this point, Lindbergh had never even been on a date with a girl. He was shy and uncomfortable around them. Soon Lindbergh became annoyed with all the attention. A shy loner by nature, he was being grabbed and touched by strangers.

The relentless attention made him sick of being a hero. He just wanted to get back to promoting aviation and getting the spotlight off himself. But it was no use.

Most of 1927, Lindbergh spent talking to airline officials about setting up regular commercial airline service. He went to a dinner with President Calvin Coolidge. There, he met Republican Dwight Morrow and his family, including his three daughters. One of the girls, dark haired Anne, took special notice of Lindbergh. He, on the other hand, did not seem to see her at all.

Later, Lindbergh flew to Mexico and stayed with the Morrows. Dwight Morrow was now ambassador to Mexico. This time, Lindbergh did notice petite Anne Morrow. She had a tiny figure. She was obviously intelligent and lively.

Anne Morrow wrote in her diary after the dinner that she liked Charles Lindbergh. But she really did not believe such a celebrated hero would ever take an interest in her. Still, she began reading *Popular Aviation.* She took a plane ride on the outside chance that Lindbergh would ask her out.

On October 3, 1928, Lindbergh called the Morrow house. He made a date with Anne. He took her for a ride in his plane, and he promised to teach her to fly.

The courtship went quickly. In February 1929 Anne Morrow and Charles Lindbergh were engaged. They were married, May 27, 1929, in Englewood, New Jersey.

Anne and Charles Lindbergh were very different people. She was well read, a good writer, and a lover of music. Lindbergh had never read a book that was not about aviation. Anne was more well educated than Charles, but they were very much in love.

Anne Lindbergh was determined to please her husband. She flew regularly with him, learning to work the radio and read charts. By the middle of 1929, she was a qualified navigator and radio operator, and then a pilot.

On June 22, 1930, the Lindbergh's first child, Charles Augustus Lindbergh III, was born. There was incredible interest in the baby, like there was about everything related to Lindbergh.

Lindbergh began to hate the **press** because they were always prying into his life. It was impossible for him to move around without news people following him. He also worried that all this publicity was dangerous for the baby. His fears were justified.

In early 1932 Anne Lindbergh was expecting her second child. The Lindberghs lived in Hopewell, New Jersey, on a large **secluded** estate.

On the evening of March 1, a Tuesday, the family was following its normal routine. The nurse put baby Charles to bed in his crib on the second floor. Charles Lindbergh had arrived home. He was downstairs working when the nurse came running to him.

The nurse had gone to the nursery at 10 p.m. and had found the crib empty. She thought Anne Lindbergh had taken the child, but she had not. Now, the nurse told Charles Lindbergh that his son was missing.

The Lindberghs began a **frantic** search for Charles to no **avail**. Then, on the windowsill of the baby's room, they saw an envelope. It was a ransom note. The baby had been kidnapped.

A terrible nightmare had begun for the Lindberghs. They paid the ransom, but the baby was not returned. For seventy-two heartbreaking days, the police followed false leads. There was even harassing mail arriving at the Lindbergh home.

Then, on May 12, 1932, a truck driver stumbled upon the body of a small child in a field. Charles Lindbergh went to the **morgue** to identify the body of his son. The child's head had been crushed.

The Lindberghs were **devastated** by the tragedy. They were then subjected to a storm of press attention. On August 16, 1932, Anne Lindbergh gave birth to her second son, Jon.

In 1934, Bruno Richard Hauptmann, was arrested for the murder of the Lindbergh baby. He was a German-born carpenter from the Bronx. It was believed that he used a stepladder to kidnap the child. He then may have accidentally dropped Charles while climbing down the ladder. The baby must have been struck in the head, and he died instantly.

In January 1935 a six week trial was held. Charles Lindbergh attended every day. Hauptmann was found guilty and condemned to death.

The kidnapping and murder of Charles Lindbergh III had a **profound** effect on Charles Lindbergh. Everything he had always hated and feared about living his life in the full spotlight of publicity had now cost him his son. His darkest fears had come to pass. His fame made him subject to endless press stories. Hauptmann had undoubtedly been inspired by them to kidnap the baby.

All Charles Lindbergh wanted now was to take his wife and newborn son away from the United States. He wanted to take them to peaceful seclusion somewhere else. On December 22, 1935, the Lindberghs sailed from New York on a passenger ship bound for Europe.

Charles Lindbergh and his wife, Anne.

In 1936 Bruno Richard Hauptmann was executed. The Lindberghs now lived in England. There, they felt cozy and safe. The English people were more reserved. They did not approach Lindbergh on the street as Americans had done. The press kept its distance as well.

Charles Lindbergh was then contacted by a United States Army official with a request. Germany, under Adolf Hitler, was rearming very quickly. Her military might was growing so much that other European countries and the United States were worried. Many feared another world war could be on the horizon.

Lindbergh was asked to go to Germany and inspect the German Air Force, the Luftwaffe. He would go as an honored guest. But, he was asked to keep his eyes open and report back what he saw. The Germans, aware of Lindbergh's fame, were delighted to welcome him.

CHAPTER 6

On July 22, 1936, Charles Lindbergh was the guest of honor in Germany. For nine days, he toured the country looking at airplane factories. He was very impressed by the advances made by German aviation. He believed the Luftwaffe was an awesome force.

Lindbergh also liked the orderly society he found in Germany. The press was considerate and respectful. Lindbergh was pleased with everything he saw in Germany.

Lindbergh had gone to Germany to find out if the developing war machine posed a threat to the rest of the world. He came away with the belief that Germany was very strong. He thought that it was so strong that engaging it in a war would be a terrible mistake.

In the fall of 1937, Lindbergh returned to Germany and became even more convinced of Germany's great power. He returned to England to convince the British to avoid conflict with Germany.

In 1937 the Lindberghs' third son, Land, was born. Lindbergh was spending most of his time **campaigning** for peace. In August, Lindbergh visited Russia. He hated the communist system being used in Russia. He was not impressed by Russia's military or anything else he saw there.

In 1938 at Munich, Britain **appeased** Adolf Hitler by giving in to his demands for more land. Charles Lindbergh thought it was the right thing to do. He was becoming more and more pro-German to the shock and dismay of many of his friends.

Hitler had been **persecuting** the Jews and other minorities for some time. Brutal concentration camps were being built. Eventually, millions would die there. Most people outside Germany believed Hitler was an evil man and a danger to humanity. Lindbergh did not see any of this.

In October 1938 Hermann Goering **decorated** Charles Lindbergh with the Service Cross of the German Eagle. He was decorated for his contribution to aviation. Goering was a Nazi leader and founder of the savage Gestapo secret police.

Lindbergh was very upset to find many people in England preparing for war. Lindbergh believed the Nazi **regime** in Germany had some good points. He felt Germany was justified in invading Czechoslovakia. He also thought Germany was an important barrier to the spread of communism.

Charles Lindbergh learned that people in the United States were also preparing for war with Germany. He was anxious to return home. He wanted to explain to the Americans how useless it was to fight a powerful enemy like Germany. But Lindbergh was worried about how he would be greeted in the United States. He knew that many people were bitter about his pro-German attitude.

Lindbergh left his family in Paris and returned alone to the United States. He wanted to make sure it was safe before he brought his wife and children home.

He landed in New York in 1939 and had a meeting with President Franklin Roosevelt. The two men distrusted one another. Roosevelt believed war with Germany was inevitable. Lindbergh believed that such a war must be avoided at all costs.

In June 1939 Lindbergh brought his family home. They lived in Lloyd Neck, a secluded part of Long Island, New York. Lindbergh then was on temporary active duty as a colonel in the U. S. Army Air Corps.

In September 1939 Hitler invaded Poland. England and France went to war against Germany.

President Roosevelt was shocked that even now Lindbergh was making speeches urging the United States not to get involved in the war. Lindbergh believed Germany would defeat Britain. To Lindbergh, it did not matter to the

United States who won. After the war, the United States could just make friends with the winner.

Lindbergh **resigned** from the U.S. Army Air Corps. He made a radio address urging neutrality for the United States. The German army was entering Paris. The Luftwaffe was bombing Britain.

In 1940 the Lindberghs' first daughter, Anne, was born. Lindbergh joined the America First Committee. It was an organization fighting to keep the United States neutral.

Lindbergh spoke to the Congress. He wanted to urge them to turn down the Lend Lease Bill. The bill was for sending war materials to help England and other countries fighting Germany.

In April 1941 President Roosevelt held a press conference. He said Charles Lindbergh would never be called to

active service because of his opinion that Germany was going to win the war.

Roosevelt compared Lindbergh to men who had become traitors during the Civil War. Roosevelt had doubts about Lindbergh's loyalty. The president ordered an investigation of Lindbergh. Lindbergh was watched constantly to see who he was talking to and what he was doing.

In May 1941 Charles Lindbergh made a speech saying that Jewish interests were pushing the United States into the war. This brought a storm of criticism against Lindbergh. Many of his closest friends and admirers turned against him.

On December 7, 1941, Japanese planes attacked Pearl Harbor in Hawaii. The debate about whether or not the United States would go to war ended with that attack.

Charles Lindbergh was broken-hearted by the turn of events. He fought hard to keep America at peace, but now he wanted to fight for his country. He offered his services to the army.

He was sent to Secretary of War Stimson. Stimson told Lindbergh that President Roosevelt considered him unfit for service because of his pro-German **sentiments**. A saddened Lindbergh looked for other ways to help with the war effort.

The Lindberghs' fourth son, Scott, was born in 1942. Around that time, Lindbergh received a call from automobile **tycoon** Henry Ford. Ford had shared Lindbergh's passion to keep the United States out of the war.

Ford had a large auto factory at Willow Run in New York. The government had asked him to convert production there from cars to military materials. Ford asked Lindbergh to help him turn the plant into a B-24 bomber producer. Ford wanted to do this as quickly as possible.

Charles Lindbergh worked with Ford. Soon, the Willow Run plant was turning out B-24 bombers at an astonishing pace. Then, Charles Lindbergh found a way to join in the war effort without President Roosevelt knowing about it.

Lindbergh's friends from the United States Navy **conspired** to sneak him into the South Pacific war theater as a civilian technical assistant. President Roosevelt was not told. It would be a secret mission.

On May 8, 1944, Lindbergh landed in the South Pacific. All he was carrying was a shaving razor, soap, boot polish, chocolate bars, a toothbrush, underwear, and a copy of the Bible.

Lindbergh's job was to train other American pilots to fly the Corsair planes in combat against the Japanese in their Zero planes. Lindbergh got aboard one of the Corsairs with a .45 automatic pistol in his gear. He was not authorized to take part in military action. But he had to be ready for whatever happened in this war zone.

During the flight, the pilot flying Lindbergh's plane **strafed** Japanese military camps with machine gun fire. Soon, Lindbergh was firing too. He flew on dawn patrols. He also helped rescue downed pilots over the jungle and in the open sea.

He always asked to get into the front lines. The Marines found out that he, a civilian technical assistant, was actually firing weapons in combat. The Marines winked at it and looked the other way.

On May 29th, Lindbergh dropped a five-hundred-pound bomb on a Japanese aircraft position. He was an expert bombardier.

CHAPTER 8

In the weeks that followed, Charles Lindbergh flew more combat missions than an average combat pilot. He dive-bombed enemy positions, sank barges, and patrolled.

Just about every Japanese anti-aircraft gun in Western New Guinea had shot at him. Lindbergh logged twenty-five combat missions and ninety hours of combat time.

On July 10, 1944, he was told that General Douglas MacArthur wanted to see him in Australia. During their **cordial** meeting, MacArthur asked Lindbergh to return to New Guinea to teach pilots how to reduce fuel consumption. This would enable combat flights to last longer.

On July 28, 1944, Charles Lindbergh joined the 433rd Fighter Squadron as an observer. The mission was to bomb and strafe Japanese positions. Soon, Lindbergh's plane was under attack.

Lindbergh fired for several seconds, watching his shells zoom through the air. But he seemed to be on a collision course with a Japanese fighter plane. As the Japanese plane neared, Lindbergh pulled back on his controls with all the strength he had.

There was a great jolt. The two planes had just five feet of air between them. Lindbergh had managed to avoid the collision by his maneuver. He watched the Japanese plane fall from the sky into the sea. Lindbergh had gotten his first enemy plane.

Lindbergh did not **boast** about the kill or his skill in saving the plane. He quietly said he shot in self defense and said little else.

Days later, Lindbergh was again in combat when a Japanese Zero dove down. The Zero fired at the tail of Lindbergh's plane. Lindbergh crouched behind the armor of the plane and expected to die. But another American plane's bullets shot down the Zero.

Friends tried to talk Lindbergh into returning to the States, but he insisted his job was not yet done. He went to Kwajalein and instructed fighter pilots in long range cruising missions. Once more he flew in combat. Lindbergh met again with MacArthur. He complimented Lindbergh on the Zero he had gotten.

In September 1944 Lindbergh flew over the Japanese held **atolls** of Taroa, Maloelap, and Wotje. He carried the heaviest bomb load ever put in a F4U. On September 13th, he dropped the bomb on Wotje Island, destroying a Japanese gun position.

With the end of World War II in sight, Charles Lindbergh ended his combat missions. He headed home. During the time Lindbergh was flying, President Roosevelt never learned that he was fighting. After all, Lindbergh was the man he had deemed unfit to wear an American uniform. But Lindbergh was serving gallantly in the most dangerous war zones.

The last Lindbergh child, a daughter, Reeve, was born in the fall of 1945. The Lindberghs moved to a secluded woodland in Scotts Cove, Connecticut. Charles Lindbergh was able to enjoy his five children. He read to them, invented games for them, and taught them to fish, sail, and hike.

He was a demanding father. He made the children perform their chores to his satisfaction. Anne Lindbergh was a much gentler parent.

All during the Lindbergh marriage, Charles Lindbergh was often away. Because of this, Anne Lindbergh struggled with loneliness. She wrote poems and essays expressing some of her feelings. She began having her articles and poetry published in major magazines.

Charles Lindbergh also turned to writing in the late 1940s. He wrote *Of Flight and Life,* published in 1948. He described some of his flying experiences. He said that he had come to understand the horrors of Nazi Germany.

He also warned against the spread of Russian communism which was causing great anxiety at the time. He urged a return to basic spiritual truths rather than a complete reliance on science.

Lindbergh always had a deep **pacifism**

in his heart. He flew combat missions and bombed targets. But he was sad to realize he was taking life. With the publication of his book, Lindbergh's popularity grew. Even those people who were critical of his attitude before World War II had a better understanding of his reasons.

Charles Lindbergh was awarded the Wright Brothers Memorial Trophy in 1949. The twenty-fifth anniversary of Lindbergh's historic flight in the *Spirit of St. Louis* was in 1952. But he refused to take part in any of the **commemorations**. His strong desire for privacy was still dominant. He did not want the searchlight of the press to find him again.

In 1952, Lindbergh published his second book, *The Spirit of St. Louis*. It told the story of the flight in 1927 and many later events in his life. The book became a best seller. It did even more to restore Lindbergh's reputation. In 1954 he was awarded the Pulitzer Prize for the book.

Lindbergh's plane, the Spirit of St. Louis

Also in 1954, President Dwight Eisenhower approved the restoration of Lindbergh's military status. Lindbergh was honored for his contribution to aviation and his great combat service in the South Pacific during World War II. He was made a Brigadier General in the United States Army. In the same year, he was awarded the Daniel Guggenheim Medal for contributions to the nation.

In 1955 Anne Morrow Lindbergh also published a memorable book. During her many years of reflection, she had written down her thoughts. They became *Gift from the Sea*. The small book became an even greater best seller than her husband's book. It remains a classic.

Charles Lindbergh was now working as a **troubleshooter** for the United States Air Force. His vast knowledge of aviation was used in the development of the nation's rocketry and space programs.

In 1927 Charles Lindbergh had flown over the entire United States, looking down at the beautiful landscape. Many times before, he had made similar flights. But, he increasingly noticed how civilization was moving in on nature. He became troubled by this.

Charles Lindbergh had always loved aviation. But now he began to wonder if the technology he had done so much to advance had really helped humanity.

In September 1962 the Lindberghs were warmly welcomed to the White House by President John F. Kennedy. They spent the night in the Queen's Room at the White House. Lindbergh was deeply moved by the president's graciousness and Jacqueline Kennedy's warmth.

CHAPTER 10

Charles Lindbergh joined the World Wildlife Fund out of his concern for vanishing species and the damaged environment. He traveled all over the world to see the effects civilization had on the natural environment.

He visited Africa, Indonesia, and South America. He joined in campaigns to save specific endangered animals. These animals included the great blue whales, the giant land tortoises, and other species. He became passionate about saving native peoples, animals, birds, plants, and trees.

Lindbergh spent a lot time with the Tasaday tribe in the Philippines. It was a small tribe that lived on the island of Mindanao. They had become objects of curiosity and were threatened with the loss of their way of life.

Lindbergh landed among the Tasadays from a helicopter. He spent some time living with them in a steep mountainside cave. These cave people had not changed their way of life since the dawn of history, and Lindbergh observed how happy they were. The jungle supported them. When he asked them if they needed anything, they could not come up with a request.

Through Lindbergh's efforts, the Tasaday area was named a national reserve. It was banned from outside interference.

Lindbergh fell in love with Hawaii. He bought a small house in Maui. In 1970 he published another book, *The Wartime Journals of Charles A. Lindbergh.* The book revived some of the **controversy** of the wartime years. He said that the world was now threatened by dangerous communism. He stubbornly pointed out that this was because of the removal of the German barrier to Russian communism.

In the fall of 1973, Charles Lindbergh, who was always very healthy, suffered from a rash and fever. The **ailment** was at first described as shingles. But then he got a nagging cough that would not go away. He went to the doctor and was diagnosed with advanced lymphatic cancer.

Charles Lindbergh had no fear of death. Throughout his life, he had not been a regular churchgoer. But, in later years, he became interested in religion. He went to a Benedictine monastery in Pennsylvania for solace in 1970. He returned there several times, deeply affected by the spirituality.

Lindbergh wanted to die at home. In the same way that he carefully arranged other parts of his life, he now planned his funeral. He returned to Maui and had a coffin made from eucalyptus wood. He decided he would be buried in a drill shirt and pants.

He chose a burial site in the churchyard. He selected the minister who would read during the service. For about ten days, Charles Lindbergh grew weaker.

During that time he said his farewells to his children and his wife. He double checked his will to make sure everything was in order. On the morning of August 26, 1974, Charles Lindbergh died. Rev. Tincher, who **presided** at the brief ceremony, described Lindbergh's death as just a new adventure.

Charles Lindbergh, as a very young man, launched the aviation age. His courageous, solo flight across the Atlantic Ocean in 1927, opened the era of commercial aviation. Aviation had been seen as a hobby of daring stuntmen. But then it was accepted as a future means of transportation for humanity. Throughout Lindbergh's life, he advanced the cause of aviation. He also contributed to the space program.

Lindbergh's opposition to America's entrance into World War II was seen as very wrong. This was especially so because of the enormous evil of Nazi Germany. Lindbergh was a brave combat pilot in World War II. But in his heart, he despised war. He believed that in the end, it accomplished nothing.

He refused to change his position, even though it almost cost him his reputation. Although he passionately opposed the war, he almost died many times fighting for his country. He was far older than most other pilots. He could have easily avoided the danger of combat.

In his later years, Charles Lindbergh remained a pioneer. He pointed out the real dangers of the destruction of the environment. He fought against rampant technology and for endangered species.

He dared to ask the question of whether the aeronautical world, for which he had given his life, had really helped or hindered mankind. He left it for others to answer the question.

Charles Lindbergh, as a young man, helped launch the aviation age.

BIBLIOGRAPHY

Berg, A. Scott. *Lindbergh.* New York: G.P. Putnams Sons, 1998.

Mosley, Leonard. *Lindbergh: A Biography.* Garden City: Doubleday and Co. Inc., 1976.

GLOSSARY

accomplish: to achieve or complete

aeronautical: having to do with the science of flight and aircrafts

ailment: sickness; illness

appease: to settle down or please

assail: to attack or assault

atoll: a ring-shaped island or reef

avail: purpose; benefit; gain

aviation: the operation of aircrafts

backers: people who provide financial support

biplane: an airplane with two sets wings

boast: to brag

brisk: chilly; cold

cadet: a student who is in military training

campaign: to work for or spread the word of a cause

coachman: a person who drives a coach or carriage

commemoration: a celebration of an event or a person

conspire: to plan in a secretive way

controversy: a public dispute or debate

cordial: polite

decorated: given metals for military service

devastate: to destroy or ruin

endorse: to show support for something

frantic: very worried; anxious

hangar: a place where an airplane is stored

hysterical: very worried; out of control

lanky: tall and thin

livestock: animals that are raised on a farm

marksman: a person who shoots well

morgue: a place where bodies are taken

pacifism: the strong belief in peace

pelt: hitting hard

persecute: to oppress or harass because of religion, race, or beliefs

pole: to move on a raft in the water with the use of a long pole

preside: to hold a position of authority

press: the media; the people who distribute news

profound: deep; powerful

pulley: a wheel that is used to increase the force that is applied to it

regime: government; command

Republican: a political party in the United States that is generally associated with conservatism

resign: to retire a position or job

secluded: hidden; sheltered

sentiment: feeling

sextant: a tool that uses the position of stars, the sun, and the moon for navigation

startle: to surprise

strafe: to attack by airplane with machine gun fire

strut: structural supports

throttle: a lever used to control the speed of the aircraft

trawler: a fishing boat

treacherous: dangerous

troubleshooter: a problem solver

tycoon: a powerful businessperson

INDEX